An Ordinary Pen.
No Ordinary Love.

Denise Meier

Presentation by *BookLeaf Publishing*

Web: www.bookleafpub.com

E-mail: info@bookleafpub.com

ISBN: 9789360943264

First edition 2024

I dedicate this book to my family and children who loved me during a time in my life when I wasn't very lovable because I was in so much pain and heartache that was primarily hidden. And it is because of the poems in this book that I am a better person and mother now because through them I cried out to God and He heard me and sent His Son Jesus to love me and heal me so I could be the wife, mother, daughter and sister God wanted me to be.

PREFACE

God told me one day that He needed a love reaction from me. He said I needed to write down how He made me feel and share it with others so you would know how to talk to Him today. Because in God's eyes, so far today is all you have, or actually only this moment perhaps, because He doesn't tell us when our last breath will be. But, for me, that ignorance is what eggs me on and urges me to write down everything I know about Him and how I feel because time is short.

And I'm no psychiatrist by any means. Actually, I'm an accountant who at the very least knows how to count and keep track of things. But I also know how to love and I've learned to love God in a way I never thought I could or knew existed. And now He wants you to know how to love Him, too, so you can have your own love reaction today and express it to Him because that's what makes Him feel happy, special and loved by you so very much. And, of course, all of this comes not by our own hand, but by the One who made it possible for us to love God, His Father, as He loves Him. And that One is Jesus Christ. So I close with thanks to Jesus for making it possible for me to love my Father in Heaven the way He does to be able to write about it. In Jesus' Name. Amen.

Table of Contents

No Ordinary Love

An ordinary pen. No ordinary love.
That's what my Father in Heaven's made of.
No ordinary light. No ordinary pang.
Rip-roaring thunder runs through my veins.
It's life all night and life all day.
It's love, joy and laughter to light my way.
It's love, joy and laughter to see me through.
Get down on your knees. He's waiting for you.
He's waiting for you to take you Home.
The Spirit God sends down from the throne.
The Spirit will teach you all that you need.
No more restrictions. No more defeat.
Only loving and laughter loud.
The Spirit of God will teach you how.
No more wondering which way to turn.
To your Heavenly Father from now on you'll
run.
He'll teach you things you've never been taught.
He'll show who He is and who He is not.
He'll tell you the truth in different ways.
There's no more defeat and no more dismay.
Then you will see the one thing that's true.
No ordinary love He gives to you.

Some Say Love

Some say love is a kiss in the night,
But I know what it is. It's Jesus Christ!
He comes to take my guilt away.
He comes to say that it's okay.
He comes to say I can do no wrong,
For underneath are His big, strong arms.
His big, strong arms catch me every time,
And tell me still I'm one of a kind.
They tell me still that He loves me.
Never will I go. Always will I see.
Always will I see His truthful heart.
The truth of it is, He'll never depart.
He'll never leave me by myself.
I love you, Jesus! You save from hell.
So make us strong and make us proud.
For we are Your children, I'll say out loud!
Yes, we are Your children. Now come to us.
Come to us so we can trust.
For if we only trust ourselves,
We're doomed for good. We're doomed to hell.
But that won't happen because of You.
I love you, Jesus, for You are true.

I Love How

I love how I hear You.
I love how I know.
I love how You tell me.
I love how we grow.
I love how You tell me that I'm number one.
Lord, You mean to tell me I matter that much?
You have so many children. How can this be?
Lord, I'm so excited about the possibilities!
What will I be and what will I know?
Who will I meet and where will we go?
But I know most of all, You love me best.
Wherever we travel, there You will rest.
There You will be fueling our faith.
Saying to believe. Your amazing grace!
For it took grace to bring us here.
Lord, I'm so glad You brought us near.
Near to You is where we will be.
Lost in love for eternity.

Finding God's Rest

Finding God's rest. Learning through tests.
Learning to pray along Heaven's way.
That's where I'm headed tonight and today.
What will I wish? What will I know?
What will God tell me below from His throne?
What will He wish for my heart to be?
Surely His love and His laughter I'll see.
Surely His love my own heart will know.
Then I can love below Heaven's throne.
For if I love on earth, God will be proud.
His love will save me. His heart will shout!
He will be so pleased. What will I do?
I will just rest and hold on to you.
It's you that I pray for. Some of you know.
Some of you know me. Some of you don't.
But that doesn't matter. God is the one,
Who knows what you need under the sun.
The sun and moon. They are all His.
All that He wants us to do is just live.
Just live and pray and learn to just love.
The rest of your life is His part to touch.

At What Point

I didn't know at what point the fear would leave,
But I prayed and it did.
It left just like that. No turning back.
No turning back to fear again.
Only love, hope and truth to start again.
Again I'll start. God promised me,
A land full of love. A heart that is free.
A heart full of love where hope remains.
The land of the free. The home of the brave.

God Said Go Through It

God said, "Go through it. Go through the trial.
I'm on the other side ready to smile.
I'll smile at you. Smile at Me back.
That's all I need. That's all I ask.
That's all I need. Love's on its way.
This love won't leave. This love will stay.
This love will stay. I promise you.
Now go through it. Love's waiting for you."

God's Great Love

God is not disappointed in me for He doesn't
look at what I am.
He only looks at what I can become.
He only looks at what I can become with the
help of Jesus Christ.
For He sent Jesus in my heart to be the Way, the
Truth, and the Life.
Jesus has touched my heart and He's teaching
me His ways.
He says I need not a man teach me for His Spirit
will lead the way.
His Spirit will lead the way to the Truth in order
to change my life.
For He didn't come to condemn me, but He
came to enhance my life.
He came to enhance my life with His grace and
His love,
And to give me power from on High to do the
things that He does.
For He chose me even in my sin.
He chose me. I did not choose Him.

Faith Says He Will

Faith says He will. Doubt says He won't.
Faith says stand still and believe and just hope.
Faith says, "I can do all things through Christ who strengthens me!"
Faith says, "Dear Jesus! I believe! I believe!"
For the faith of a tiny mustard seed is all that He requires,
To move in His love for you, for you are His desire.
And when you believe in Him, His heart is filled with joy!
And when you learn to trust Him, oh how the Heavens rejoice!
For there is no greater love than the love He has for you.
No, you did not choose Him. Instead, He chose you!

Yes, Jesus Saves

Yes, Jesus saves and Jesus heals.
You need to know that He is real.
And He will come right when you call,
For He is near to you, never far.
The way you walk, the way you talk,
Will all be changed in the blink of an eye.
He wastes no time to make you right,
For in His heart you are His delight.
And when you're down, He'll give you love,
For He sure knows that you've had it tough.
And if you know that someone cares,
Then in your heart, you will not despair.
But in His arms, you'll learn to trust,
That Jesus saves, no He's not like us.
Yes, Jesus saves and Jesus heals.
You need to know that He is real.

Thoughts On The Lord

He doesn't blame me. He changes me.
He doesn't scold me. He holds me.
He doesn't whip me. He lifts me.
He doesn't leave me. He keeps me.
He doesn't lie to me. He cries for me.
He doesn't threaten me. He protects me.
He doesn't cheat me. He gives to me.
He doesn't ignore me. He talks to me.
He doesn't bind me. He frees me.
He doesn't harm me. He tests me.
He doesn't wound me. He heals me.
He doesn't starve me. He feeds me.
He doesn't sadden me. He gladdens me.

The Race Of Faith

The Good Lord says I don't have to have a
system or plan in place,
For he has set a course for me and now I just run
the race.
But the race is one of faith, He says, and trust
like I've never known.
And in this race I'm running, He says, He's
beside me and guiding me Home.
Home is where Jesus lives and where angels
rejoice on high.
And Home is where my Heavenly Father is and
where He looks down on me from the sky.
Because Jesus says my Father knows this great
race I have begun.
And He will set my feet high upon a Rock where
it will be easier to run.
Yes, this Rock is named Jesus and He will run
with me through every test.
And He will help me overcome every obstacle
for I am running with the Best!
You see, He knows the race I have to run
because He's laid it out for me.
"And by the way," the Lord says, "This race is
set to set you free!"

It Wasn't Up To Me

It wasn't up to me. I did what I had to do.
I gave my heart to God. I forgave you, too.
He asked me to love and never look back.
He asked me to give if even not given back.
All this I did do. My conscience is clear.
The years are all gone. The sadness disappeared.
Today is God's day. It's new if you want.
Today is the day our God's giving His love!
Do you want that love? How about me?
I'll take that love in a New York heartbeat!
But now it's your turn to love and react.
To let our God teach you there's no turning back.
For yesterday's gone. Who wants it anyway?
I sure don't miss all the pain and the pain.
For that's all there was. Pain and despair.
Now it's time to let it disappear.
Let it all go. It's not up to me.
It's all up to you to decide to be free.
But God is right here. Know this for a fact.
That whether you sin, He will still love you
back.
So run to Him now. It's never too late,
To give Him your heart. Don't make that
mistake.

Don't make that mistake. Please give Him your
heart.
Today is the day for a brand new start.

No Fear

Lord, what is it like to have no fear?
To never be frightened? To never shed those
tears?
What is it like to know You best?
To know who You are? To pass all Your tests?
Where do You want to take me today?
What do You want and how do I pray?
Show me how to get to Your heart,
So the root of all evil will quickly depart.
For if I am all flesh, I don't stand a chance.
But when Spirit comes, it's the victory dance!
For the devil can't get to me anymore,
'Cause with You by my side, it's victory galore!
It's only victory and never loss.
It's only victory over my heart.
For my own heart deceives me today.
It tells me to look at the world, not pray.
But I know that's wrong. I've been through Your
tests.
I've been through enough to know You know
best.
So now I ask You to deliver my heart,
From my own visions and my own thoughts.
Now it's time for You to come in.

The way that You are. The way it should've
been.
'Cause I don't like the way this feels,
To not be at peace because pain is real.
And when I'm in pain, I know it's not You.
But I know it's time to run to the Truth.
'Cause You tell the truth, never a lie.
You always tell me the reasons and why.
And then You say to worry no more,
'Cause forgiveness with You is an open door.
And I don't have to feel the shame,
Of coming to You with a heart that is stained.
'Cause all of our hearts are stained with regrets.
With knowing the truth but doing the opposite.
So that's why now I can say with relief.
I'm glad I know Jesus. My chains He breaks
free.

A Life More Surrendered

A life more surrendered.
Listening to God and learning to pray for what
He has planned.
Wondering when He'll answer and watching His
Hand.
"Sit back and watch how I do it," He says with a
grin.
"Remember I told you that love was gonna
win?"
"We are gonna win!"
A life more surrendered.
It's doing it all for the glory of love.
Wondering sometimes is this real or am I nuts?!
It's hoping in God that He will repay,
The love that He died for. The grace that He
gave.
A life more surrendered.
Looking at myself.
I wouldn't trade it for the world!
What can compare to God's wealth?
A life more surrendered.
It's mercy and grace.
In times of great need,
He's a healing face.
A life more surrendered.

It's looking at me.
The person I've become.
Who I wanted to be.
A life more surrendered.
It's looking at everything through God's eyes,
not my own.
But it's calling grace my own because He gave it
to me,
To have and to hold until death do us part.
My Saviour I owe a life more surrendered.
That's all I owe and that's all He wants.
A life more surrendered to love, shape and mold.
It's me by His side to have and to hold.
My life more surrendered.

He's Building Them A House

He's building them a house.
A house that's built on love.
More than you can imagine.
More than you can dream of.
But this house it will take some time,
To be what it needs to be.
But in it you can rest assured,
Will be love and family.
Yes, He's building them a house.
This house it's already done.
Only fun, food and laughter,
And all the joy a child dreams of!
So what is best to do?
It's best to wait and see.
For soon you'll see what God can do,
He can create a family.
So don't give up too soon,
Or you'll miss this house for sure.
So listen as He's saying,
Complain less and trust Me more.
Otherwise, you will regret it.
It's as simple as two, three, four.
And then this thought will plague you,
I should have waited and trusted more.
For God's plans are for your choosing.

They're not to be thrown aside.
For only a fool would do this,
Not seeing his anger and pride.
But God is full of mercy.
He'll beat you to the cross!
And there is where He'll tell you,
Leave your anger and let's move on!
For there is more at stake here,
Than selfishness and pride.
You risk to lose your family,
And the home I have supplied.
So what is best to do?
Repentance is the best.
It's best to tell Me your mistakes,
And I will do the rest.
For there's no grudge in Heaven.
Forgiveness is for sure.
Now let's get on with this old house,
Before My blessed return!

Fiery Eyes And Dreams

With fiery eyes and dreams no one could steal,
God dreamt of a family that He could heal.
He dreamt of a way that they'd understand,
That He was their forever, faithful friend.
So He took them away to His heavenly home,
To show them His seat upon the Throne.
And there He taught them very well,
To love their neighbor, each other, themselves.
For who would have thought they knew no love.
But born of the Father, they learned to trust.
And soon they saw what they'd never seen.
The faithful cross missing something.
For Jesus no longer hung on that cross.
He died for their sins and then He came off!
He rose to prove deep in the night,
That He is faithful and all is bright.
So the next time you see a cross in the way,
Remember it's Jesus who's come down to stay!

When Worry Left

When worry left, it was peace galore!
On a piggyback ride we walked on the shore.
I hopped on His back 'cause the walk was too long.
And that's what He wanted me to do all along!
'Cause that's what a Daddy does, He said.
He'll carry you home when you're exhausted.
But before I would walk alone, by myself.
Thought I could do it needing nobody's help.
But then that day came when I needed some help.
The water was high and I was drowning myself.
I tried to swim but it wasn't enough.
It left me breathless wanting to give up.
Then the Saviour came and lifted the load.
He taught me to swim very well on my own.
But now I swim to Him for help.
When the tide is high there is someone else,
Who will pick you up when you are down.
Who will pick you up so you won't drown,
He'll teach you how to run to Him.
You'll run on the water never falling in!

Lord, Why Me?

A lot of the time you ask in your heart,
Lord, why did you choose me to play this part?
Why did you choose me to do your will?
Look, Lord, at me. I'm so broken and frail.
Well, says the Lord, I choose those in their sin.
Don't you remember that I rose again?
I rose to defeat the devil in your life.
I rose to give you power and might.
I rose to prove that even in your sin,
That you can be chosen to succeed and to win!
For the Lord is on a mission to save your soul.
Yes, to regain it and have full control,
From the enemy, the devil, and all of his darts.
And from his plan to destroy you and ruin your
heart.
For your heart belongs to the devil no more.
And as you surrender, I will make you pure.
For I am your refuge in time of your need.
So come to Me with your sin so I can set you
free.

When You Haven't Got A Prayer

When you haven't got a prayer in your heart to say,
I pray that my prayers will light the way,
To the Father's heart and to the Father's soul,
And into His mind so that you will know,
That Jesus loves you with all of His heart,
And from your side He will never depart.
Because He knows your sorrow and He knows your pain.
Yes, He knows it well for He has called you by name.
He knows your prayers when you have no words.
He knows your heart and your desire to serve.
And He will make a way when others say no.
For He will show them who is really in control!
And He will not leave you stranded in grief.
No, He will pick you up and get you back on your feet.
For we serve a God who is greater than all.
And He will come quickly even before you call.

In Case You Didn't Know
What To Pray

In case you didn't know what to pray,
I said a prayer for you today.
No, I didn't always know what to say,
But I just knew that I had to pray,
And ask the Lord to prove to you,
Just who He is and what He can do.
To change your heart and change your soul.
To make you well and make you whole.
Because Jesus loves you more than you know.
And in His time you shall quickly grow.
And come to see Him just as He is.
So don't be afraid because you are His.
And He has plans for you and your life.
For you are His daughter, His friend, and His
wife.
For He is the Bridegroom and you are the Bride.
And He has come to stand right by your side.
So in your trouble run quickly to Him.
For He is waiting on you to seek Him.

Learning To Fly

Learning to fly.
Lord, I don't know why.
Why did you pick me?
Look, Lord, I'm so weak.
Look, Lord, at my house.
It's so messy. I'm not proud.
Lord, I need your help.
Help to heal and help to help.
Help me help my heart,
To not carry things that aren't.
Things that aren't my burden.
And things that are an intrusion.
Things that intrude my soul.
Things that make me low.
For, Lord, this learning to fly,
Sometimes makes me cry.
It's true stress at its best.
It's things that take my rest.
But, Lord, that's not your way,
To leave me alone all day.
So take this worry and doubt,
And bring your heavenly shout!
And make my wings to stay,
In precious flight all day.
So I can stay above the burden,

That comes to try to ruin.
To ruin my visions of Heaven,
And take away my blessing.
To shoot holes in my wings,
So I can fall, not sing.
So today I'll sing to Heaven,
'Cause God has fought for blessing.
Even though He didn't have to,
He took away my statue.
The statue of sin that stood,
In my way for good.
The statue of sin that stared,
And looked at me in despair.
For now I've learned to fly,
And He is the reason why.
I love you, God, my Dad,
For Jesus makes me glad.
I love you, Jesus, loud.
You make my heart feel proud.
I'm proud to be your daughter.
I love you, Jesus and Father.

The Best Dressed

There once was a great Kingdom she heard so
much about.
"Who will let me in?" she said. "How much is
the amount?"
All those who were around her were the best
dressed of the best dressed.
Perhaps the King would let her in if she also
dressed the best.
Was this the way to please Him? Had she found
the way for sure?
Then suddenly the King shouted, "No! Come as
you are!"
"See, that's the mistake that people make. They
think they have to please Me.
But I say come as you are. Let Me do all that's
needed.
For I am the one who dresses you in fine linen
laced with gold.
For all the other dresses you'd wear are only as
filthy mold.
And in My clothes you'll surely be the best
dressed of the best dressed.
For all My clothes are guaranteed with love and
righteousness.

And these are the things I'll dress you in. I know
that you'll be pleased.
And all of this I'll clothe you with right there on
bended knee."

Rest, My Sweet Darling

Why do you mourn?
Now celebrate life!
Do what you have to.
Make that sacrifice.
For I am there with you.
I love your long hair.
Never do I leave you.
I stay right there.
Right there will I trust you.
I'll show you the way.
Now it's time to work.
Later it's all play.
For Heaven's My homeland.
It's vacation galore!
Never will I leave you.
I'll meet you on the shore.
For you love the water,
The ocean and tide.
And there will I meet you.
Right by your side.
I'd teach you to swim,
'Til the oceans run dry.
But you have been given,
Great wings to fly.
So fly to Me, darling.

Come near to My nest.
For you have been chosen,
To fly above the rest.
So rest in My Presence,
And know that I'm near.
Now rest, My sweet darling.
Your Saviour is here!

Brave New Girl

Long ago, a Man wrote a story.
It was about a brave new girl.
He showed her truths of a different kind,
And presented her to the world.
What was she to do with all this truth?
"Go and tell it!" He said from the roof.
"Go and tell it! Tell them I save.
Tell them I'll heal them. Tell them I'm brave.
And because I'm brave, you are, too.
Don't be troubled about what you're to do.
Just go do it 'cause I am there.
Soon they will see there's no despair.
For I took it from you. From you they could not.
They don't control you. They're tied in a knot.
They don't control you. I am the One,
Who answers to heaven, for I am the Son.
So please come and know Me. I promise I'm
there.
Please come and touch Me. My heart won't
scare."

Ways That I Heard Him

Ways that I heard Him.
Ways He prepared.
Ways that I loved Him.
Ways He stayed near.
Ways that He loved me.
Ways yet unknown.
Ways that He hugged me and carried me Home.
Ways that I wondered, "Why me, true Lord?"
Ways that He answered, "My love is sure."
Ways that He told me, "Your love's the best!"
Why? 'Cause I trust Him. My heavenly rest.
Ways that He showed me His love is real.
Ways that He told me. Ways that He healed.
Too many ways He tells you the truth.
Only to heal you. Only to prove.
Only to show you His way is best.
His way is promised God's heavenly best.

The Best Sleep

The best sleep I ever got,
Was when I saw what God was not.
He was not my enemy on the Throne.
He died on the Cross to take me home.
He died on the Cross to marry me,
So I could love and I could see.
He died on the Cross so I could abound,
In love, hope and grace and everything sound.
In love, hope and truth and everything new,
To start off your day with His love to you.

Mommy Got Healed Today

Mommy got healed today. I bet you didn't
know.
All that time spent on her knees will really really
show.
All that time spent on her knees was only all for
you.
So she could be the mom you want, the friend
and comrade, too.
Yes, mommy got healed today. I bet you are
surprised.
Never doubt in God above. His wonder never
dies.
"Was mommy always sick?" you ask. "I could
never tell."
Yes, mommy had some pain inside that God
threw into hell!
Today He threw that junk away. He didn't waste
no time.
"Today is all we have," God says. "Today is
always Mine."
So would you rather laugh real hard or cry those
selfish tears?
Would you rather cling real hard to happiness or
fear?

I'll take happy. You take sad. It's really up to
you.
But sad is not what I have planned. What I have
planned is new!
New, new life and new, new breath. There's
nothing more to say.
Do you want this life of Mine or shall I give it
away?
Many men would die for this. One already has.
One has paid the price for you for this new life
to have.
Jesus Christ has died for you. Now all you do is
ask.

I've Come A Long Way

I've come a long way in this 'ole fight.
I've learned what was wrong. I've learned what
was right.
I've learned that the place where true love
comes,
Is from God's open heart and God's only Son.
I've learned that the way to love and to give,
Is to ask for more grace. The sky's the limit!
I've learned that I don't have to love all.
Only those that my Father one day died for.
He sent His own Son to die for my sins.
But, me, I didn't notice. I didn't give in.
But one day Holy Spirit came down for a dance.
He came down to show me the two-step prance.
One step to the right. Two steps to the left.
Now you're closer to getting God's best.
Now that you listen, you can hear Me.
It's amazing what you hear when you stop
talking!
Now can you hear? I'm well on My way.
I'm coming to show that My promises stay.
I'm coming to show that I love you best.
The Best of the Best brings sure promises.
Now will you trust and not lose your peace?
'Cause those that love Me ain't missing a thing!

This Is Gonna End

This is gonna end. I just don't know when.
This mountain's gonna move. God promised me
that, too.
This mountain's gonna go straight to hell where
it belongs.
'Cause that's where it came from when fear had
me strong.
For the devil is there, but angels stand,
In the devil's way at God's command.
They protect our heart and protect our soul.
They protect us when we shouldn't know.
For we should have never known hate in this
world,
For we are of God. His heavenly pearls.
But because we're here 'cause man did fall,
God fights for our hearts the fiercest of all.
He loves our hearts with all His might,
'Cause that's what He sees all through the night.
He sees our hearts give up in despair,
So He comes to us and shows He cares.
He loves us more than words can say.
The Bible is just a taste of what awaits!
That's what I heard God say today.
And this is gonna end 'cause I have prayed.

I'll Give You Tonight

I'll give you tonight to get over your fears,
But just know in the morning I'll be right here.
I'll give you tonight to get over your fright,
But just know that everything's gonna be alright.
Why? 'Cause God loves us and He never lies.
And the promise He's made is that you will
survive.
Even times you don't think so. Even times that
you cry,
God is always right here to wipe tears from your
eyes.
And to tell you He loves you. To tell you He's
nigh.
Nigh, nigh. God is always nigh.
Nigh means near and He's near you tonight,
To tell you to wait on His promise of light.
He'll light up your way so that you can step
right.
So that you can now see all that's caused you
this fright.
So that you can tear down all that hinders
tonight.
So that you can see God in His glorious light!
Light, light. God is shining above,

And down does He come to show you His great
love.
Love, love. That is all that He knows,
To comfort your heart and comfort your soul.
And tonight He has promised His love you will
know.
No more despair. No more no hope.
Only His love that will grow in your soul.

Girl Interrupted

Hey, girl interrupted. Let the past be the past.
It's no longer your sin. It's no longer your sash.
For you wear your sin like a weight on a rope,
Tied around your neck. Always tied to your
hopes.
Who lied to you in your moment of fright?
Who came to you and said all is not right?
Well, it wasn't right but I came anyway!
I came to take trouble and sorrow away.
Hey, girl interrupted. It's Me can't you see?
It's Me telling You to love Me, only Me!
For I was there with you. I left you right there.
To show you the truth. To show you I care.
For if all was all perfect, then you wouldn't see,
What I can do and what I can be.
For I am there near you starting each day.
I am there near you. Please won't you pray?
So you can stop listening to their foolish words.
Yes, you still listen though it was fifteen years
ago.
Though they are not speaking, you hear anyway.
Your heart still remembers. The pain still pains.
So now let's think different and holy, you see.
'Cause holiness says that you are worthy.
I died for your sins for you to have life.

So you wouldn't have to. So you could survive.
But it's not just surviving, it's living, you see.
To you, I give life more abundantly!
So hold on! Get ready! Here we go!
Hold on! Get ready for nothing you know!
For you don't know life, only sorrow and pain.
But if you hang with Me, it's time for the games!
For I like to play like little boys do.
I like to dance. What about you?!
Hey, girl interrupted. Now can you see?
That those in My hand ain't missing a thing!
For they will all have My life and life more.
My Father in Heaven says to hold back no more!
Isn't that something? God's open door!
And what comes from it will make your heart
soar!
There's no looking back. You're ahead of the
game.
Quickly, now hurry, for true love awaits!
It's time for the games to begin then you'll see.
The reward of the Father for believing in Me.
For it is so simple. Don't make it so hard.
Only believe and you will go far.
Your husband, he hears you. He's not far away.
Please don't be worried. His heart won't stray.
For he longs to see you and tell you some more.
That he really loves you and he'll change for
sure.

So please now believe Me and know in your
heart.
That My life is in you. Now let true love start.
It's no longer you you will see anymore.
It's My Holy Spirit you'll see from now on.
So believe in this promise and don't be afraid,
Of what true love is. It's how Heaven was
made.
And Heaven is where all the little girls play.
No more interruptions. No more delay.

She Used To

She used to be sad. She used to be mad.
She used to not wonder in God as her Dad.
She used to not know His love and His grace.
Would she go to Heaven or stay in this place?
For this place was hell. This place was her life.
Her life was left beaten and broken inside.
Her life was her heart. God gave it to her,
So He could now tell her how much she was
worth.
To Him she's worth gold, but she couldn't tell.
For she was believing the lies from hell.
The lies they will come for Satan is good.
He's good at the lies when you're
misunderstood.
He'll tell you you're dirt or much worse than
that.
He'll tell you God hates you and not coming
back.
His tongue is a knife he sticks in your heart.
So please don't believe him for God is at large.
Yes, God is at large inside of your home.
Your home is your heart. His heavenly throne.
That's where He'll come and rest for a while.
He'll never leave if you give Him a smile.
Show Him you care and want Him to stay.

He'll teach you to love and teach you to pray.
He'll show you He's kind and happy to be,
There in your heart. His Spirit makes three.
And where Jesus is, God's Spirit is free.

Daughter

Daughter, I have a mission for you.
It's one of faith and possibility, too.
It's one of hope. Can you withstand?
The love that I have? It's not like a man's.
My heart is real. My heart is true.
I'll never tell lies. That I won't do.
I'll break through your heart and throw hurt
away.
So My love can grow and My love can stay.
Then you will see that purity lives.
From My heart it comes. To your heart I give.

Somehow

Somehow I go to sleep every night.
Somehow it doesn't bother me then.
Somehow God is always there to remind me,
That He's gonna win in the end.
Somehow I go to work and work.
Sometimes not wanting to be there.
Sometimes my heart hurts so much.
That's when God comes to heal it.
Sometimes I wonder, "Is today, Lord, the day?"
"Will my prayer get answered? Will his heart
stay?"
Maybe today will be good. Maybe I'll let it be.
God has taught me to pray and trust.
Hurry, hurry love come to me!

Day by Day

Day by day. What will God say?
What will He do or introduce?
What will He want from my own soul?
He'll call for peace and a gentle soul.
He'll call for truth that you must speak.
Never a lie or vain deceit.
For all is well on heaven's row.
It's death for you but life for your soul.

Strong in Faith

Strong in faith. Free of doubt.
No more trying to figure it out.
Strong in hope. Strong in love.
Strength from Heaven, from up above.
No more fear. No more doubt.
No more trying to figure it out.

Thinner

I feel thinner.
Less burdens. Less load.
The Lord is breaking my yoke.
Thinner is as heavy was.
No wonder I could never run!
It was too heavy.
Now light on my feet. No more deceit.
Thinner has come to bring me peace.
Do your job, oh thinner, proud!
Take the heavy. Take the loud.
Bring to me a cup of peace.
A lighter load. Now I can breathe.
Thinner.
It feels so good to be thinner.

Trials Along The Way

Trials along the way.
We watch and we pray.
What will God do?!
What will God say?!
We wait so excited for You, our dear Lord.
What will You say from behind Heaven's door?
How will You feel and how will You be?
Me, I just know You will act graciously.
Me, I just know You will do what is best,
To teach us Your truth, Your joy and happiness.
Me, I just know that You are the One.
You're God's own vision and Heavenly Son.
You're God's own vision for the world to be.
Please help us, dear Father, tremendously.
Now help us, dear Father, so we don't run,
Away from our problems and away from Your
Son.
Please help us, dear Father, for we love You
best.
These trials along the way are Your perfectness.
These trials along the way are for us to know,
Your wonderful power and wonderful glow.
For glory is there if we will but endure.
And weeping for the night, it will stop for sure.
For glory comes and Joy shows its face.

Look! It's God smiling! My sins He's erased!
Look! It's God smiling! He's always been
there,
To rush to your trials. For your soul He cares.
He cares so much that we would die,
If He wasn't right there through the day and
night.
So trials along the way, they're not so bad,
As long as God loves us and takes our hand.
As long as God loves us, we're well on our way,
To what Jesus calls Heaven where children play.
Where children sleep 'cause there is no harm.
That's where we're headed embraced in God's
arms.

My Heart vs. His Heart

Lord, You're so different than me.
Make me to be like You.
Help me to be like You.
Help my unbelief.
I pray for Your character.
I pray for Your heart so faith can start.
I pray for Your truth so You can unloose.
So you can untie the noose.
The noose around my neck that restricts the
Spirit.
The noose around my soul that blocks Heaven's
flow.
Oh Lord, make me to be like You,
Because it's a sad thing when hearts aren't true.
Because Your heart is always true.
Yes, it's always true to You and who You are,
Because You can't betray Yourself. From You
lies are far.
For You are the Truth where lies don't exist.
As if the Heavenly realm would let hellish lies
in.
God forbid!
No, in Heaven only Truth exists.
And if I have Your heart, Your truth will come
in.

Something Already Prepared

Something already prepared.
That's what God wants to give you.
Can you accept it? Will you take it?
Will you take it and take care of it,
Or turn and run the other way for what people
might say?
Will you need it and love it?
I know you will and I know you can,
'Cause you're a very special woman and man.
More special than you think.
In Jesus' Name. Amen.

Where Courage Lives

Where courage lives, lives strength to heal.
Strength to conquer. Strength to feel.
Where courage lives, lives lots of rest.
Lots of truth and happiness.
There lives no doubt. There lives no fear.
Only Jesus standing near.
So always carry courage proud.
It'll save your heart and let out a shout!

What Would Touch Him Deeper

What would touch Me deeper is for you not to
worry.
What would touch Me deeper is for you not to
blame.
What would touch Me deeper is for you to let
Me,
Prove who I am and the power in My Name.
For I am Jesus. I'm Jesus Christ.
I'll heal your wounds and I'll heal your fright.
I'll heal your heart and all it's made of.
I'll heal your greed and say that's enough.
I'll tell you this and tell you that,
Then I'll follow through and that's a fact.
Yes, I'll follow through. This you should know.
That what would touch Me deeper is in your
soul.
For what would touch Me deeper is already
there.
Now let it come out and begin to share.
Yes, let it come out and love your life.
For I'm Jesus Christ. No more strife.

Our Jealous Lord Speaks

"Maybe I want you to cry for Me like you cry for him.

Maybe I want to feel wanted and needed and then I'll speak.

I'm calling to see if you still need Me. Do you still need Me, Denise?"

Lord, of course, I do! I'm sorry I don't say it enough.

What am I not saying to You enough?

Please help me and form those words in my heart to say to You.

"I want you to say that without Me you can do nothing."

Lord, without you I can do nothing!

"I want you to say that you need Me with all your heart."

Lord, I need you with all my heart!

"I want you to say that you will love Me forever."

Lord, I will love you forever.

"I am satisfied and I love you with all My heart."

I Feel Something

I feel something letting go and behaving.
For my flesh is contained and there's no more
fear.
I feel God.
I feel something settling in my bones.
The Presence of God only Heaven knows.
No more fear. Only relief.
No more pain.
Only God to gain.
And why does the flesh hate me so?
It's 'cause it's got no place to go.
Only to hell, not to heaven.
The flesh is against all that's well.
So that's why God comes to laugh,
At my tribulations and trials at hand.
For He now says to patiently wait.
The future's at hand. It's not too late.

It's Been A While

It's been a while since someone said,
I'm a beautiful woman and a beautiful friend.
It's been a while since I felt real.
I felt so used. I felt like steel.
Would I ever feel again,
The touch of a husband who's a lover and
friend?
Does that exist? I'd ask my God.
I'd plead with Him to stop the facade.
For things were hidden no one knew.
Things were hidden that made me blue.
But now I know what true love is.
It's honesty and hope and bliss.
It only comes from hearts that feel.
It only comes from pain so real.
For when your heart's been broken in two,
You listen more and look for clues.
You look into a person's heart,
To find yourself. To find a start.
You look to start all over new.
You wonder if God's following you.
Well, yes, He is! He's here right now.
To heal your kiss and heal your smile.
He's here to come and carry you,
Away from sin and all you knew.

For knowing God means many things.
It means you're clean. It means you've
changed.
It means you're headed somewhere new.
It means that God's forgiven you.
It's been a while since you heard that.
Now rest, my child. No turning back.

The Opposite of Faith

The opposite of faith is being double-minded.
You either have faith or you don't.
You're either gonna go all the way with God or
you're not.
It's that simple.
It's like trying to do two things at one time.
You can't!
Neither can you do anything without God.
So just trust God, okay?
Your mind is here and your mind is there.
Your mind is wondering and your mind is
praying.
Just pray!
Yes, just pray and your mind will be at rest.
Amen.

Unto Us Little Children

Oh, dear Jesus, why do I try and understand?
Why do I try to figure You out when my life is
in Your hands?
How come I want to know everything before it
comes to pass?
Why do I think I need to prepare my life when
my life is in Your hands?
Why do I think I need to know what others think
of me?
Why do I care so much when they turn and
make fun so happily?
Because You said when they mock me they're
really mocking You.
But if they only knew You, dear Jesus, they
would be sad and blue.
Because then they would realize whose feelings
they were really hurting.
But I don't wish harm on any one person.
No, I just pray that they would know You.
And learn to love You, love me and others like
You do.
So their life can be happy and full of joy and not
so sad and blue.
Because what they do unto us little children,
they really do unto You.

So instead of passing judgment, dear Father, first
give them a chance to know You.
Because then I'm sure they would come to terms
with the way they've treated me.
And instead of making fun of You now, they
would want to be part of our family.
For God so loved the world that He chose to
give His only son.
That whosoever believes in Him will not perish
but will live in abundance.

What's So Special

What's so special about this day?
It is special 'cause I have prayed.
It is special 'cause I have seen,
God at work and God planning.
For He has planned to come real soon,
To take my heart from where it looms.
For there are times when I get scared.
But Jesus says, "No more despair!"
Yes, Jesus comes to do what's right.
He heals my heart all day and night.

Spiritual Things

Who can explain spiritual things?
It's too much for us but for God it's nothing.
It's nothing for Him to give us His love.
In Heaven, He waits for our prayers to touch.
They touch His own heart and God only knows.
The way that He loves us. The way that it
shows.
He does many things. Things we can't see.
So don't ever wonder if God is trustworthy.
Him you can trust today and tonight.
He tells you He loves you. The moment is right.
He takes every chance to show you He cares.
Soon you will see there's no heart of despair.
Where did it go? Your sadness is gone.
God came from Heaven and brought joy along.
The joy that you have, God gave it to you.
So you could be glad and start seeing the truth.
The joy that you have, it drives away hate.
The person you've hated is you. Did you
think?!
But now that God comes. You'll learn to love
you.
And God will be happy there's no more blues.

If I Really Knew You

Father, if I really knew you, I don't think I
would ever cry.
Only tears of joy, I think. Never tears of despair,
For I would know that you've come to heal and
share.
You share Your glory with me. The Spirit's
glory of love.
You let me take from You so I can give it to
others.
I'm really starting to know You and it feels
really good.
I know You defend my honor when I'm
misunderstood.
I know You stand by my side when others stab
me in the back.
They can't see they stab You, too, but the knives
we don't throw back.
We just pray and let the Father do,
All that He's good at. He's happy to.
He's happy to take our burdens away,
So we can be free to love and play.
The Spirit plays. He loves to dance.
Just follow My lead and take a chance.
Just follow My lead to where no one goes.
I promise you we're headed Home.

I promise you that all is well.
Heaven is coming to shake up hell.
Yes, heaven is coming. Don't hesitate.
My Father is strong. My Father is brave.
You've done real good. Now learn to lead.
For I'm in front, in back, in between.
I'm everywhere. You'll never escape.
The way that I love you. My lady afraid.

Upon The Wings of Love

Waiting on the wings. Upon the wings of Love.
Where will God's Spirit take me? What will my
soul learn of?
What will my soul now dream? I'll leave it up
to God.
What will my soul now see? No more sad
facades.
For truth is bound real tight. On earth, it's
meant to be,
Loosed into your heart for all the world to see.
And once the world has seen God's truth inside
your heart,
They will know of Jesus and they will know of
God.
No more can they say that God is not right here,
For truth inside your heart reveals He's very
near.
So let it be to them a sign of things to come.
For you, it's just to wait upon His wings of
Love.

I Think About You, Lord

I think about You, Lord. I think about Your life.
I think of how they stabbed You with a speary knife.
I think of how they gloated with coldness in their eyes.
"How could God allow this?" You thought to my surprise.
I thought You had no feelings. That's what churches teach.
All they ever want to do is take and take and preach.
But have they suffered with You? This I do not know.
But if they have You promised me their works would really show.
For these last days, You're coming. You're coming with surprise.
Nobody can run from You and nobody can hide.
So help my heart today, Lord, and help me promise You.
With Your help, I promise You my heart is always true.
True to You today, Lord. Please keep it strong and clean.

Strong for when the devil comes with hate and
faith testings.
Keep me strong like Job, Lord. Curse You he
did not.
And when his trial was over, his blessing was a
lot.
You blessed him more than ever for faithfulness
and love.
Now help me, Father, help me. Show me what
I'm made of.
To me, that's very scary. I'm starting to now
see,
That everything that's weak in me You must
now make it leave.
But how do I survive, Lord? You look for love
that lasts.
Amidst the trials and testings, who'll give You
the chance?
The chance to get to know You. Lord, it must be
me.
And everything that's weak in me in Jesus'
Name must leave.
For nothing's for my doing. You do all the
work.
All You say for me to do is trust and trust and
trust.
Trust You with my life, Lord. Trust with family.
Trust You with the things inside that no one ever
sees.

Lord, You'll never shame me. Proud You are of
us.
Proud You are of those who come and trust You
with their stuff.
Stuff can mean their money or things in life they
have.
Would they really trust You if Satan came and
laughed?
Laugh at us he does, Lord. He calls us zealous
fools.
If loving You means I'm a fool, I know not what
I do!
I'm glad to be a fool, Lord. A fool in love with
You.

So Still

So still are God's ways. I sit here amazed.
He keeps me abreast. He loves me the best.
He loves me in truth. Lies just won't do.
They'll never reveal His love that's so real.
How does He do it? How does He know?
How can God see straight into my soul?
What does He find there? Sometimes I'm
afraid.
Will He forgive the mistakes that I've made?
To Him there's no question. It's already done.
It's already planned. It's already won!
Please, don't you want it? Love and His grace?
Please now come get it. Don't hesitate!
Please come to God. He's waiting for you.
His ways will amaze you. His heart is so true.
His loving will shock you! You'll wonder why
me?
How can God love me? My heart's so filthy.
But that doesn't matter. To Him you are pure.
To Him sin is nothing. Your heart He adores.
Your heart He will cleanse. Your troubles will
go.
And soon you will see that life of His grow.
You'll grow in His arms. Gosh, He loves you!
You are His child. He'll carry you through.

He'll carry you through with love and His grace.
"Be still, My child," He'll say to your face.
"Be still, My child," He'll whisper to you.
"Hurry, now hurry. I'm waiting for you."

It Is Done

It is done. Jesus, come.
Please bring me back from where I have run.
Please bring me back to inner peace.
I've run too far. There's no more relief.
I've run too far from Your sweet grace.
I've failed too much at saving face.
All You want is honesty.
Please help my pride so I can be free.
Please help my pride so I can know,
That I am saved by grace alone.

Mrs. Mercy

Mercy's waiting to be given at your front door
today.
But when you open the door, you don't know
what to say.
Surely you've got the wrong door. My neighbor
is down the street.
But Mercy doesn't move a bit. She just falls
down at your feet.
Let me in! Let me in! Because you don't know
what you're missing.
I'll huff and I'll puff and blow away the
condemnation.
Who is this one called Mercy who runs swiftly
to my door?
She's a daughter of my Father and He sent her to
restore.
And she'll restore what's missing for now and
forevermore.
So welcome Mrs. Mercy when she comes
knocking at your door.

Who Are You, Lord Jesus?

Who are You, Lord Jesus, that You're mindful of
me?
The closer I get to You, the more that I see.
That You are the Way, the Truth and the Life.
And I am so shallow, so weak and full of fright.
But You say I can do all things through Christ
who strengthens me.
Oh, Jesus, my Saviour, help me to believe,
That there's nothing I should fear with You by
my side.
Yes, help me to stand tall when all I want to do
is hide.
I get so scared that I don't know what to do.
But I remember You telling me to run quickly to
You.
So I run to You, Jesus, for comfort and strength.
I run to You, Jesus, because You take all the
blame.
You take all the blame for my sins and my fears.
And You teach me to love You as You wipe
away my tears.
I don't understand You but I've come to believe,
That the battle is not in my hands. It is won on
my knees.

Yes, prayer is the answer to all things great and
small.
And to know that You hear me is the greatest
gift of all.
I love You, dear Jesus, with all of my heart.
Who are You, dear Jesus? Please give me Your
heart.
For what is in my heart will come out of my
mouth.
And I want others to know You so help me to
shout.
That You are the Way and the Truth to me.
Because when they see my life I want them to
believe.
So make me an example of Your love and Your
truth.
And help me to endure for Your word You want
to prove.

First Walk A Mile

First walk a mile and then you can judge.
Then you can hate her or then you can love.
Then you can know how she really feels.
Maybe she's broken underneath all that steel.
Maybe she's broken. You don't even know.
Maybe it takes her forever to show.
Maybe it takes her too long to write,
'Cause she can't tear away from the evil fight.
For Satan he has her just right where he wants.
He wants her right there where she can't throw a
punch.
He wants her right there exhausted and blind.
But little does he know that God has her mind.
Yes, God has her mind and fills it with truth.
He fills it with hope and faithfulness, too.
He fills it with joy that loves her real well.
Joy tells her to wait for strength to come dwell.
For strength comes real quick. It's a matter of
fact.
If you'd walk that first mile then you would
know that.
Yes, you would now know how God loves her
well.
That's why she can win when others have failed.

That's why she goes on 'cause God's got her
back.
If you'd first walk that mile then you would
know that.
Then you would first love and be slow to judge.
But you can't know all this until your mouth
you've shut.
Then God can begin to show you her heart.
And then He will help you take the hate out of
yours.

I Never Knew That I Couldn't See

I never knew that I couldn't see,
Until Jesus shined His light on me.
I said, oh Lord, oh Lord, why did you choose
me?
Because I can't see in me what You see.
He said, my child, I choose those in their sin,
Because the devil has blinded you deep from
within.
You think that this is the life for you.
You think that my plans are so far and not true.
I have to get you to believe the devil no more,
Because he is a liar for real and for sure.
And he robs you of the peace that I have for you,
Because lately you have been so sad and so blue.
Why do you cry so much from within?
Don't you remember that I rose again?
So stand with your heart so tall and so true,
Because I know that you love Me and I love
you, too.
And this is not the life that I have for you.
No, I will make you believe in love once again,
Because you have been deserted by an unworthy
friend.
He left you on the corner so naked and so shy,

And all you could think of to do was cry.
But I heard your tears and I've come to rescue
you.
So calm all your fears because I see all things,
too.

Fasting For Change

I'm fasting for change. I'm fasting for me.
I'm fasting for something I don't see.
I'm fasting for life. I'm fasting for death.
I'm fasting for all of God's breath.
I'm fasting for hope. I'm fasting for truth.
I'm fasting for whatever will change you.
But most of all, I'm fasting for love,
'Cause that is what God is made of.
Love for you and love for me.
Love for the way we want to be.
Love for whatever is in God's plan.
He'll take us by the heart and take us by the
hand.
We'll land in a place we've not been before.
But it is beautiful. Yes, beauty galore!
It's peace and quiet, truth and hope.
It's all things we couldn't do on our own.
So now what do we do? We wait on God.
For He is lovely and not very far.
He hears our hearts when we have no words.
He tells our souls to trust in His word.
So now we're here and God is there.
Maybe before you didn't care.
But now you do. I see it good.
I see your heart coming up from the dirt.

For God has breathed His life into you.
So take it, child. It's yours to use.

Silence Makes A Sound

Silence makes a sound. It says to wait on God.
No more sad deceivers. No more sad facades.
No more wondering when. You'll give it all to
Him.
Then you'll watch Him coming to you riding
down from Heaven.
He'll ride down on His horse. His horse of
pearly white.
He'll come to you in visions and dreams all
through the night.
He'll come to you with love. Yes, that's His
specialty.
He comes to you with love and grace to teach
you to believe.
'Cause once you feel His touch, He says you're
sure to turn.
You'll turn around and run to Him and meet Him
on this earth.
For God is close right here. He's walking in our
land.
He's looking for a few good souls to save men
from their sins.
He's looking now for you. Will you hear His
call?

Come now! Come now! Run to Him! His
heart's not very far!
It's right in front of you. For if this you now
hear,
That just tells me more and more your salvation
is near.
And soon you both will dance. And God and
you will sing.
You'll sing a song of lovely love and grace and
beautiful things.
You'll sing a song of truth. No more lies or
fake.
No more wondering what to do. In silence,
you'll have faith.

Seeing Her In Pain

Seeing her in pain, Jesus wept the same.
Seeing her great need, Jesus walked the sea.
He came to her from a distant land saying,
My child, I understand your hidden pain.
My child, I understand your longing heart.
Now trust in Me for a brand new start.
Now trust in Me for everything.
My heart is glad. My love is free.
My heart is glad to serve you well.
I'll never leave. It's heaven or hell.
It's heaven's door for those who choose,
A better life. That's My good news.
But hell is left for those who run,
Away from God and from His Son.
So choose it wise. Choose God today.
And He will wipe your tears away.
Yes, He will wipe the pain that's real.
And give you joy for this new year.

Her Justice

Her justice came. It was not in vain.
Not a moment too soon, God came through.
Not a moment too loud, God made her proud.
Love she did choose. God brought truth.
From His Book of Truth, God brought good
news.
Good news here and good news there.
Truth and mercy everywhere.
Favor came and stole the day.
Favor came and wisdom prayed.
Wisdom prayed. God took the chance,
And rescued me from circumstance.
No one thing should take your peace.
Fight for it! Yes, fight for keeps!
For God took the chance and sent His Son,
To die for you. His chosen one.
He took the chance you would believe,
In Jesus Christ for all your needs.
He took the chance for you to know,
That He's your Father and He loves you so.
For you are chosen to believe,
In Jesus Christ for eternity.
And Jesus Christ will serve you well.
His justice will come to shake up hell.
His justice will come to you and your life.
For you have been asking for no more strife.
And our Mighty God sees everything.

For He is the Judge of the dead and the living.
So go in peace and live your life,
For God's defense is your heavenly right.
And others will reap what they have sown.
And God will tell them to leave you alone.
And far away from you will they be.
As Jesus Christ tells them to leave.
For His commands are firm and loud,
In the spiritual realm where His love abounds.
For Jesus has the final say.
And justice for you is on its way.
Yes, justice for you is in His plans.
Yes, justice for you is in God's hands.
On judgment day we're all gonna be the same.
Won't matter who knows who.
Only matters if you know God.
Do you?
Only matters what your heart wears.
Is love there?
Only matters if you speak the truth.
Did you?
Only matters if you know God.
Did you know His Son Jesus, too?
So pray, pray before judgment day,
For it is sure to come without delay.
Pray, pray for sins to be washed away,
Says God and His Holy Son this day.

Pushed As Far As I Can Go

Pushed as far as I can go.
When will it end, Lord? When will I know?
When will this trial be far from me?
Lord, now I see You! Lord, now I can see!
It will be done when You are done.
Contrary to nature, I should have fun.
Fun in my trials, God is telling me.
Fun in my heart will set me free.
For joy is there. How bad do I want,
To be free from anger, hurt, and lust?
How bad do I want that heart of His?
As bad as vanilla loves chocolate!
As bad as God does love My heart.
He loves the way I pray real hard.
He loves the way I go through things
Pushed as far as I can go? You ain't seen
nothing!

She Writes

He created an environment for her to write.
Through her husband, yes.
But it was God, nonetheless.
He liked what she wrote.
Her pen she did stroke.
But it was God's words.
She wrote things that she heard.
She loved what He said.
He spoke life and not death.
She'd open her ears and He would appear.
Write what you hear. Write what I say.
Doesn't matter if they think that way.
Write what you know. Never stop My flow.
For Spirit is strong and Spirit is deep.
Holy Spirit won't stop even while you're asleep.
So go with God's flow for Spirit is there.
Inside, outside, everywhere.
For God is around. Believe it or not.
If they will believe is up to you not.
Just say what I say with no more despair.
Look up, look down, for God is there.

Write These Words

Trust in the Lord with all your heart,
And lean not on your own understanding.
Father, write these words on my heart today.
Make them stay and play and dare to dream.
Make them soar down from Heaven and attack
my heart.
Yes, this would be a good heart attack.
Your words attacking my heart!
Consuming me.
Using me.
Yes, using me to do Your will.
Oh, dear Father, I get chills!
I get chills just thinking about You.
Yes, all that You see and all that You do.
With You there are limitless possibilities.
With that in mind, how do I believe?
How do I believe in a God that is true,
Not to mention huge?!
How do I believe in a Daddy's touch?
For You are my Dad whom I love so much.
How do I know if I'm believing right?
Come, Lord, dear Jesus. Take away my fright.
Come, Lord, dear Jesus. I'm believing well.
I believe You take souls out of living hell.
For hell is living all around us.

And because of that You hurry and come.
For You have a job to do at this time.
It's to rid our souls of the evil that hides.
It hides in our heart. You know that so well.
That's why I thank You for loving me from
There.
For there You sit beyond Heaven's gate.
You're never far off nor are You late.
No, You're right on time so I need not fear.
Lean not on my own understanding. Make this
real.

Shake Gently

Shake gently, my Lord. My heart is not well.
I've just learned of Heaven and evil hell.
I've just seen the light. It's not what I thought.
Today I saw Jesus and my life He bought.
Today I saw Jesus on top of God's throne.
He said with a shout, "My people come home!"
My people come home 'cause there's not much
time.
Only time for salvation and the gift of life.
Only time for love. Only time for truth.
Only time for the Spirit to untie your noose.
'Cause until you found God, you choked on His
Word.
But now through confession, the Spirit returned.
Yes, now through confession, the Spirit is back.
It's as simple as this and as simple as that.
Not many realize that that's all God wants.
A heart that confesses and doesn't just run.
So don't run away when sin falls in your lap.
Just take it to God and His grace He'll give
back.
Just take it to God and forgiveness He'll give.
His love He will show so that you can live.

Where Have I Been, Lord?

Where have I been, Lord? In hell with all its sin.
Thanks for getting me out. Thanks for coming
in.
Thanks for reaching low and catching my lost
heart.
It's run so far from you. It's run so very far.
Now what do I do to chase the fear away?
Lord, you would not save me to hang me the
next day.
Please, Lord, I'm so scared. Is this sin beneath
Your grace?
Have I gone too far? My life I have disgraced.
Now I come to You 'cause You, Lord, came to
me.
Teach me how to be the child I need to be.
'Cause you said I'm your child and there's no
need to fear.
All I need to do is keep You very near.
So now, Lord, when I run, please pull me back
real soon.
Don't ever let me think that I know more than
You.
But teach me, Lord, Your way and soon we both
will see.
The woman I can become through grace and
liberty.

A Picture Of You

God showed me a picture of you.
'Twas a snapshot of two. You were happy, not
blue.
You were happy in love with a man who was
kind.
His love and affection kind of blew your mind.
For in your past life, you weren't treated so well.
The husband you had was a bat out of hell.
He was mean and rude and greedy, too.
He never cared if you had enough food.
He never cared how he hurt your heart.
But God always saw and gave you a brand new
start.
Yes, God always saw. He saw your kind heart.
He saw you loving others while you were
distraught.
He saw how you loved though you were not
loved back.
Now God is the one blessing you for all of that.
For He saw the way you would give and would
give.
Now He says it's time for you to just live.
Just live in your love and your happiness, too.
'Cause, you see, God is faithful to women like
you.

Yes, women who love and women who dance.
Women who stay strong when they don't feel
glad.
Women who prove that life is one shot.
No time to be sad. God loves you a lot!

She's Nobody's Fool

She's nobody's fool. God sets the rules.
He tells her to stay. On her knees, she should
pray.
He tells her to wait for victory at hand.
It's Heaven's own heart that's come down for a
dance.
It's Heaven's own heart through the Spirit that's
seen.
Through God's lovely heart his own children are
weaned.
He tells them, "Stand strong for I made you no
fool.
This glory of Mine you will prove and will
prove.
And soon they will see that my happiness
comes,
To those who will wait and stand strong in the
Son.
For I don't expect you to stand on your own.
Your own strength will fail you. In Mine you
will grow.
For My strength will take you up high in the sky.
And there you will sit on My left and My right.
There you will sit. I'll give you the strength.
You're nobody's fool. That don't even think!

No, don't ever think they get over on you.
If they ever did then I'd be the fool!
Yes, I'd be the fool but that I am not,
For I am your Father. Your heavenly God.
So go with My flow and soon you will see.
They are the foolish ones. No, not Me!
And if I let them hurt you My love won't be
true.
I promise, My love, that you're nobody's fool."

If I Die Tonight

Today I thought of life and death.
Who can understand or make sense of it?
Who can know how long they'll live?
That's why today I'm writing this.
I want you to know that I love you.
And if I've ever offended you.
I am sorry. Please this know.
I never meant to hurt your soul.
I only meant to be of help.
To help you when you needed it.
I only meant to smile at you,
And make you feel glad instead of blue.
For we've had our problems. Yes, we have.
But our strength shined through to get through
them.
I'm proud of my family and the friends I've
made.
I want you to know for all of you I pray.
Just know in your heart that I love you.
If I die tonight, I'm glad you knew.
My kids, you mean the world to me.
I'm sorry for my inconsistencies.
But I hope you saw God changed my life.
He did it through my Saviour Jesus Christ.
And I hope you know God loves you, too.

He trusted me with the three of you.
And that just simply blows my mind,
That God would trust this heart of mine.
For I was so young those years ago,
When I thought my life was under control.
But now it's the best because you're my kids.
Ellen, Brandon and Brad, you show me God's
heart exists.
For how could He make three people so perfect?
You're perfect for me and you're God's beloved.
So if I go Home before you do.
Just know in your hearts I'll be waiting for you.
And if you start to miss your mom,
Just open this book and feel God's arms.
For He will comfort your broken heart.
'Cause He wants you to be happy and not fall
apart.
For time is short on this earth where we live.
This life is temporary. Heaven is our
homestead!
So live your life as best as you can.
Leave the rest up to God until we meet in
Heaven.

Family Acknowledgements

Mom, thank you for your faith and raising us to love and know Jesus. The devil is afraid of you still so keep the faith and keep praying for us because we need it daily as you know! Thank you for your sacrifices over the years to take care of Dad and us, and for being a mother to my children when I couldn't be properly or needed help. But now because of your faith and prayers, I am a loving, godly mother and I thank you. You are healed in Jesus' Name.

Dad, thank you for your love and generosity. You are the biggest giver I know and that only comes from the heart of God which you have. You have overcome such adversity while still keeping a smile on your face and a laugh in your heart and that speaks to us more than you know. We need that daily to show us that God is real and that He will never leave us or forsake us, so keep smiling and laughing, please, for the joy of the Lord in you is our strength!

Danny, thank you for being on this marriage journey for 16 years. Wow, has it been that long?! The devil has been attacking us from the moment we said "I do" and we are finally starting to see the light at the end of the tunnel. God's light! And I don't know who God is going to take home first, but if He takes me first, I hope the poems in this book continue to draw you closer to Jesus and His love for you because what He has spoken to me is for you, too, because we are one.

Ellen, you are sunshine on a cloudy day! And though you have had your share of clouds, the sunshine broke through every time, didn't it?! I thank God for your life and the melody He put in your heart to sing and dance at will even when nobody else is watching because that's who you are, and singing and dancing through life is what you do best! I thank Michael for working hard to provide a good life for you both.

Bradley, you are everybody's friend! God has given you a kindred spirit to draw others unto Himself in these last days because the Bible says He is a friend who sticks closer than a brother and that describes you perfectly. You have His heart to love and give which is truly the heart of Jesus. You give of yourself daily to the youth and young men and women God has placed in your life. Because of that God's plans are to reward you openly and I can't wait to see what that looks like because I know it will be good and grand!

Brandon, you are God's fire in the face of our enemy, the devil, and you have truly overcome him by the Blood of the Lamb and the word of your testimony. You are truly a walking miracle and nobody who knows you can say that anybody changed your life but God. He has set your life in motion to be a greater witness and testament to His love, mercy, and forgiveness so others will be drawn to His love, as well. Jesus loves you with an everlasting love and He laid down His life for you so you could be where you're at today which is delivered, healed, blessed, and a loving father to Zaeda. To God be the glory in your life for the way He transformed you from one minute to the next which still blows my mind and keeps me asking Jesus to this day, "Who are You?!" The way He has transformed the life of Alexus is truly amazing, as well, and I pray He touches her heart more through this book.

Brittany, I pray for you, Cameron, Lily, and Gavin everyday and I hope the poems in this book introduce you to Jesus and His love for you so you can share it with your family always.

God made you a mother and He doesn't make mistakes. The only mistake would be to not realize that you are a good mother so never tell yourself that you aren't because you are. God bless you and keep you and your family always.

Debbie, I pray for you daily and for the light of God to shine on you and through you speedily like never before because He loves you and you need to know that. He hasn't forgotten about you and He still has a plan for you, Dru, Haley, and Taylor greater than you could ever imagine.

Linda, you are God's fierce warrior who never backs down from a fight so stay strong, mighty soldier, because I need you to battle the devil with me now more than ever so I can hide behind you sometimes like I did in high school when the mean girls were mean to me! Maybe you didn't know that but you always stood up for me when I couldn't stand up for myself. You were my courage when I was afraid and I learned from you more than you know how to be strong and brave. Kaylin and Kamryn are blessed to have you as their mother and God will bless and keep them and your grandchildren because of you.

Stefanie, I put your name last for a reason and that is because you have carried this family in your heart and prayers more than we know even as a little child, but now it's time for us to know! Thank you to you and Jay for always being there for my kids when I couldn't be when I was so caught up in stupid worldly things that didn't matter. Thank you for praying because it was your prayers that brought me back to the arms of Jesus which is where I needed to be in order to be truly loved which is what I know you want for me more than anything. Thank you for being courageous enough to fight the devil on my behalf and for seeking deliverance and healing for my family. I cannot describe how much God loves you! It is beyond all human words I could even fathom to put together but He loves you and your heart of faith tremendously! He has chosen you to be the Joseph of our family to be put in the palace of His Kingdom to bring us there, and it is your love and prayers that did just that and continue to do so. Preston, Madison, and Jason are blessed and highly favored because they have a mother like you and God is with them always and will never leave them or forsake them.

Well, this is my family and my life wouldn't be my life without them. They have all made my life better in so many ways. If I could end this book with just one piece of advice it would be to tell you to forgive and love others quicker than I did. I held so many grudges over the years because of hurt and I thought I had a right to until God told me I didn't. He helped me to not only forgive others but to forgive myself because that is important, too, so you can move on with your life and from everything holding you back. God knows you don't want to be held back anymore and the first solution to that is to forgive so you can be forgiven and your heart can heal. Once you do that, you will be able to experience the extraordinary love Jesus has for you and others and you will stop living in the lowly, ordinary place of unforgiveness, for the love and life of Jesus is a place that few people truly find, but it's waiting for you if you want it. My hope is that the poems in this book helped you get there. Sweet Jesus, may you now open Your heart to each reader like never before and lift them up in Your love and truth where they belong. In Your precious and holy Name, I pray. Amen.